An Introduction to Coping with

Obsessive
Compulsive Disorder

An Introduction to Coping with

Obsessive Compulsive Disorder

2nd Edition

Lee Brosan

ROBINSON

ROBINSON

First published in Great Britain in 2018 by Robinson

1 3 5 7 9 10 8 6 4 2

Copyright © Lee Brosan, 2018

The moral rights of the author has been asserted.

A CIP catalogue record for this book
is available from the British Library.

Important note
This book is not intended as a substitute for medical advice
or treatment. Any person with a condition requiring medical
attention should consult a qualified medical practitioner
or suitable therapist.

ISBN: 978-1-47214-014-2

Typeset in Bembo by Initial Typesetting Services, Edinburgh
Printed and bound in Great Britain by Clays Ltd, St Ives plc

Papers used by Robinson are from well-managed forests
and other responsible sources.

Robinson
An imprint of
Little, Brown Book Group
Carmelite House
50 Victoria Embankment
London EC4Y 0DZ

An Hachette UK Company
www.hachette.co.uk
www.littlebrown.co.uk
www.overcoming.co.uk

Contents

About This Book

This book will help you overcome your obsessions and compulsions. The common name for these problems is 'obsessive compulsive disorder', or 'OCD' for short. The book starts by explaining what OCD is, and then goes on to talk about what you can do to help yourself overcome it. There are a lot of different variations of OCD, and so some bits of the explanation and the advice are likely to apply to you more than others. For instance, if cleaning or checking is your problem, then the section on 'Behavioural Treatment' will be very important for you; if your problem is more to do with how you think, then the section on 'Cognitive Treatment' might be more what you need. Although it would probably be useful to read everything to get the total picture, you shouldn't feel you must do this – much better to dip into the bits that seem most relevant than to be put off by the bits that don't!

To overcome obsessions and compulsions you need to work hard and persevere, and at the beginning it can be very difficult indeed to believe that it's going to be worthwhile. But when people do force themselves to make changes, the improvement can be truly amazing. Making changes takes great courage, particularly when you're starting out, but it does work!

Don't feel that you have to get everything right first time. Overcoming obsessions and compulsions is a bit like starting to exercise – at the beginning it feels like torture and you can only manage to do a bit, but as you carry on it will start to seem easier and you'll be able to do more.

This book is designed for you to use on your own. However, you may find this is just too difficult. If you can't get started, or if you don't make as much progress as you wish, then don't despair, and don't feel you have failed. You could try reading it with someone you trust, such as your partner, a parent or close friend, as this may help motivate you. Otherwise, talk to your GP who might be able to prescribe medication that can help you to make the changes described here, or refer you to your local Psychology Services – these are still in short supply in some places, but they are increasingly available, and with the right therapist you can make great strides forward.

Lee Brosan

Part 1: ABOUT OBSESSIONS AND COMPULSIONS

1

So What Are Obsessions and Compulsions?

There can't be many people in the world who have never had ideas they found weird, or done things knowing that they were silly. How many of us have ever left the house and thought, 'Did I just lock the front door?' and gone back to make sure? Or stood on a platform waiting for a train or Tube and thought, 'What if I just jumped off?' How many people avoid the number thirteen, or walk round ladders rather than under them? For most of us, thoughts like these come and go without troubling us too much. For some people, though, the ideas do not go away, but take hold of them and their lives.

This book is about what obsessions and compulsions are, and what keeps them going. It gives you specific guidelines about what you can do to help decrease the anxiety that obsessions and compulsions cause, and reduce the effects they have on your life.

Obsessions, compulsions and obsessive compulsive disorder

Basically, an obsession is something – usually a thought – that makes you feel very anxious. Sometimes these thoughts take the form of images or pictures in your mind rather than words; sometimes they are impulses or urges – a sudden feeling that you might go and do something, usually something awful.

A compulsion, on the other hand, is usually something that you do. Compulsions make you feel better, or help you feel sure that the thing that you fear is not going to happen. Usually compulsions are obvious behaviours, but sometimes they may be things that people do in their heads to try and make things 'all right'.

If these problems continue, and start to take over your life, then it's likely that you have what is known as obsessive compulsive disorder, or OCD.

A feature of OCD is that you begin to avoid the things that bring the obsessions on, and so you end up severely limited about where you can go, what you can do, who you can meet, and so on.

Is OCD common?

Recently there seems to have been a growing awareness of OCD. Magazines, and even television programmes, are featuring it. As a result, people find it easier to go to their doctors and talk about their symptoms. At the moment about 1.2 per cent of the population of the UK have OCD. This is less than the number of people who are anxious or depressed, but it's still pretty high.

What about the different types of OCD?

Although everyone with OCD has some things in common, there are distinct subtypes of the condition. These are the common ones.

Cleaning

One of the most common forms of OCD is the fear that you may come into contact with contamination of some sort, and as a result may become ill or die, or may pass on an infection and the risk of illness to someone else. As a result, people with this form of OCD spend extraordinary amounts of time washing themselves and cleaning things around them. Common things that people fear may be contaminated are food, public toilets and blood – anything where 'germs' might linger. People may also go to great lengths to avoid touching things that might be contaminated. It is not uncommon, for instance, for people to throw away huge amounts of food because they think it may be 'off ', or to refuse to eat anything prepared by anyone else.

Checking

Another very common form of OCD is checking. This may involve checking lights, plugs, electrical goods, cookers, doors, windows and many other things. It can also include checking work that you have done – it may be very difficult to finish something because of the impulse to go back over it repeatedly. An increasingly common form of checking involves driving: people have to retrace their routes to make sure that they haven't hit anyone without knowing. Checking obsessions can lead to extreme forms of behaviour, such as going round the same roundabout four times, or even ringing the police to make sure that an accident hasn't been reported.

Cleaning and checking are both very tied up with the idea that you might be responsible for causing harm to somebody, or to yourself.

Intrusive thoughts

Sometimes the main problem in OCD is the presence of unpleasant thoughts which just pop into your mind. These are often about sex or violence, or about causing harm to others, especially children. The thoughts are usually horrible and repulsive to you. But the harder you try to avoid having them, the worse the thoughts seem to get. Although there are no obvious compulsions in this form of OCD, people may have more subtle ways of coping, particularly by avoiding situations that might trigger the thoughts.

Order and symmetry

If you have this form of OCD you probably want to make sure that things are done in exactly the right way, and that objects are in exactly the right place. This may mean doing ordinary things such as washing or shaving in a particular sequence, which *has* to be done right before you can do anything else. If this is disrupted, then you almost always have to start again from the beginning. Sometimes these rituals are accompanied by counting particular numbers, which assume a great significance in your life. Or you need things to be arranged in a carefully ordered or symmetrical pattern, and get agitated and upset if they are moved even slightly. You may need to spend a long time checking that things are 'right' before you can do anything else.

Obsessional slowness

Obsessional slowness can occur when you want things to be 'just right'. Everything has to be done in exactly the right way, and all decisions have to be absolutely right. You may think that something terrible will happen if you make the wrong decision, and you need to be completely sure you are making the right one, even if this is something as ordinary as choosing what to wear. It can take a very long time to carry out simple everyday actions – even getting dressed can take a couple of hours if you need to be sure that everything has been done in exactly the right way.

Hoarding

Hoarding is a less frequent form of OCD, but can be extremely disabling. You may not be able to throw away the smallest thing – junk mail, used tickets, old newspapers, even food past its sell-by date. The fear underlying this seems to be that you might throw away something important. Hoarding can take over your life completely, as rooms and even your whole house become filled with clutter that can't be removed.

Combinations of symptoms

You may experience more than one kind of obsessional symptom, although usually one will be stronger and more of a problem than the others. Sometimes the form of OCD shifts from one type to another.

Related problems

If you have OCD you may have other problems too. You may get depressed because of what the OCD is doing to your life. Anxiety is a very big part of OCD, and sometimes OCD may be misdiagnosed as an anxiety disorder. On the whole, though, the presence of time-consuming compulsions makes it clear that this is OCD rather than, say, a 'germ phobia'.

Sally's story

Sally is a young mother of thirty-three. She went to university after school, and in her late twenties met Martin, a structural engineer. They married after a year, and when their first baby was born Sally decided to stop work for a few years and concentrate on looking after the children. Becca is now four and Ben is one.

Sally's trouble started quite soon after her daughter, Becca, was born. She noticed that she was finding it very difficult to keep up with all the washing that one small baby seemed to generate, and as Becca got older she worried a great deal about what her daughter should eat and what she should wear. Then Ben came along; the birth was very difficult and Sally knows that he nearly died. She felt very low and inadequate for some time afterwards, and the obsessions and compulsions really got out of hand.

Decontaminating children

Sally worries greatly that the children will come into contact with dirt and germs and will be made ill as a result. Becca is now at nursery, and mixes with other children there. Sally is terrified that she will 'catch something' through using the loos at nursery. After she collects Becca from nursery she takes her straight upstairs to put her in the bath. While the bath is running, Becca stands on the bathroom floor. Sally takes Becca's clothes off and puts them all into a plastic bag. She ties this up and puts it outside the bathroom door, then washes her hands with antibacterial soap before picking Becca up and putting her in the bath. While Becca is in the bath, Sally washes over the bathroom floor where Becca and her clothes had been. Sometimes Ben is awake and wants to get into the bath, too, but Sally cannot let him because the water may contain traces of germs that are being washed off Becca and she does not want them to contaminate him.

When Becca has had her bath Sally gets new clothes from the airing cupboard and dresses her. Sometimes she looks at the clothes and can't feel sure that they have not brushed against anything contaminated on the way from the airing cupboard, so she'll put them aside and get new clothes out. Then she'll put Becca and Ben in front of the TV to watch a video while she deals with the washing. She will have run the washing machine on empty as preparation earlier in the day to make sure that it doesn't contain anything contaminated. She takes the washing out of the plastic bag, wearing rubber gloves, and puts it in the machine. She has to be very careful that the washing does not touch the sides of the machine, or she will have to wash these down too. She throws the rubber gloves away. When the washing is done, she takes it out very carefully so that it does not touch anything else; the problem is that she uses the same washing machine for Martin's clothes, and because he often works on site he is likely to have come into contact with a lot of men, and she knows that men are 'not too fussy about what they do when they use the loo'.

Sally is afraid of contact with any 'dirt' from other people and from the world around her. She is terrified that her own hands may be contaminated, and has to wash these repeatedly before she touches anything, particularly things to do with food or with the children. She washes her hands using antibacterial cleaner, and when she feels desperate will also use bleach. Her hands look very red and raw, and the skin is split between her fingers, but she cannot stop washing them.

Handing over responsibilities

Sally's also starting to worry a lot that something will go wrong in the house. It's all right when Martin is at home, because then she goes to bed and lets him take over.

But if he's away she has to check everything very carefully before she goes to bed: the gas cooker to make sure that it's off and there won't be a fire in the night; the taps to make sure there won't be a flood; the windows to make sure that they are properly shut. It has now got to the point where she's making excuses not to go out in the day because she knows that it will be so difficult to leave the house and feel OK about it. This checking isn't as much of a problem for her as the washing, but it's making life very difficult.

'I know it's silly but I can't stop'

Sally knows a lot of what she's doing is silly, and in some ways she knows it would be better not to do it. But what if she let the children come into contact with something contaminated and they became ill, or worse? It would be her fault. It's up to her to protect them and keep them safe – if she doesn't, then she is a terrible mother. It makes no difference to her when Martin says, 'But no one else does what you do, and their children are fine.' She knows that the measures she's taking are extreme, but she can't take the risk.

Derek's story

Derek is sixty-six. His wife died several years ago and he lives alone in the marital home. He has one son who lives in New Zealand. He visits his son and his family every year, and they communicate quite frequently by phone and email. Derek has just retired. He's chairman of the local bowls club, and he's keen on opera. He has always taken an interest in local charities, and now helps with fundraising. He's glad to have time for these activities but is finding it difficult not being at work, and is really a bit low. He's a reasonable-looking man, and is kind and helpful to those around him. But he is starting to have a lot of very bizarre thoughts. When neighbours come into his house, he looks at knives and scissors and thinks, 'These are for stabbing.' He's got used to cooking for friends, but now he can't hold a knife while someone else is in the room in case he uses it to stab them. He has had to put the knives and scissors, and indeed anything sharp, away out of sight because he's so frightened by the thoughts they produce. He can no longer have people around for meals.

The first time he had a thought like this was last year in New Zealand. He was playing with his grandchildren, whom he loves, and suddenly had an image of himself pushing his grandson off his bike into the path of a car. He's horrified at himself, and can't understand why he should think things like this; he's desperately afraid that there's an evil side to him that wants to hurt and damage people. He can't look in the mirror any more because he's afraid that when he does, he'll see himself, not as he has always looked, but as a horrible Jekyll and Hyde figure who'll look as evil as he thinks he must be to be having these thoughts. He has started to shave without a mirror now!

He likes to believe that he's a good, decent man but he's finding it much harder to believe that now he's having these thoughts. He has to believe they're just thoughts – he doesn't mean them.

Why Do People Get Obsessive Compulsive Disorder, and What Keeps It Going?

Nobody knows exactly why some people get OCD and others don't. There may be a number of causes.

Biological factors

Genetics

It's possible that people may inherit genes that make it more likely they will develop OCD. If one or more people in your family have OCD, then this may be why you have it, but it could be because you have 'learned' OCD from seeing how someone close to you behaves, so it may not be the direct effect of genes.

Brains and biology

It's also possible that there are differences in the brain chemistry of people who develop OCD that make them more likely to develop this disorder. In Chapter 4 you'll see that there are certain drugs that work on the chemicals in the brain and seem to help people with OCD.

Psychological factors

Although biological factors may play a part in the development of OCD, there are also important psychological factors that can affect whether you have it or not. In understanding how these work, it's helpful to think about obsessions and compulsions separately to begin with.

Where do obsessions come from?

We live in a world that is often stressful and difficult. We want to stay safe, but threats to our health and physical safety are all around us – illnesses, road accidents and so on are all too common. We want our relatives and friends to stay safe, too, and we would feel bad if we did anything that might put them at risk. So we start to worry about what we are doing – was the meat we bought from the supermarket today really OK, or has it gone off? Could we have knocked into someone when we were driving home and not noticed? Did we leave the TV plugged in when we went out, and if we did, will there be an electrical fault and will the house burn down? Did we have horrible thoughts about someone, and if we did, what does this mean?

Most of us are familiar with such thoughts, but can deal with them without too much trouble. We eat the supermarket meat; we know we couldn't really have hit someone without noticing. We feel a bit anxious, but the anxiety does not rule what we do.

For people with OCD, however, something very different happens, and this is where compulsions come in.

How do compulsions work?

Compulsions develop as a way of coping with anxiety. When you have a worrying thought like, 'Is the meat off?' you decide to throw it away. When you worry that you might have knocked a pedestrian down, you go back to check. Even if you know in your heart of hearts that you're being silly, you can't resist doing it, *just in case*. And doing it makes you feel a lot better. You don't have to worry any more. This is a key point: *compulsions are aimed at reducing distress*, or preventing some dreaded event or situation – and they work! You feel less anxious. The event you feared has not happened.

So you convince yourself that you really needed to obey the compulsion – if you hadn't, you might have gone on feeling anxious for ever. Or you might have poisoned your family, or burnt the house down.

Psychologists have known for a long time that when you carry out an action that makes you feel better, *you keep doing it.* So, every time you carry out a compulsion, your behaviour is made stronger because you feel better as a result of doing it, and you are likely to do it more. But the sad truth is that, although compulsions make you feel better in the short term, *they do not work in the long term.* The more you act on compulsions, the more you need to. It might have been that when the OCD was starting you only needed to check something once, or wash your hands carefully once. But as time goes on this simple reassurance stops working and you need to do things more and more in order to feel better, until you are almost completely out of control of what you do. This is the case even if the compulsions you carry out are things that you do in your mind rather than in the outside world.

This is known as the 'behavioural' explanation of OCD – how your behaviour (i.e. carrying out the compulsions) keeps the OCD going. But there are also very important aspects of thinking (the 'cognitive' aspects) that keep OCD going.

The role of thinking in OCD

There are a number of very important aspects to thinking in OCD.

Making judgements about your thoughts – 'thoughts about thoughts'

People with OCD often have thoughts that make them feel very anxious, or which they feel are absolutely horrible. If this happens to you, you may judge yourself very harshly. Indeed, you hate yourself for having the thoughts, and think you are a bad and horrible person. Or you think that because you can't control your thoughts you must want to have them, or must be weak because you can't stop them. You try very hard to control your thoughts in a desperate attempt to make sure that they don't happen.

Responsibility and blame

People who develop OCD tend to have very strong ideas about responsibility. If you suffer from OCD, you are likely to feel totally responsible for what happens in the world around you, particularly to close family and friends, but sometimes to everyone else too. You believe that if something goes wrong it'll be your fault and you'll be blamed – you might even feel you deserve the blame simply because you are such a bad person. This very strong sense of responsibility and blame makes it very difficult for you to take risks. You can't risk going out without checking, because you are totally responsible for what might happen.

Thought-action fusion

This snappy title helps us to recognise that there is a difference between thought and behaviour. This happens when there is a muddle in someone's mind between what you *do* and what you *think* – i.e. there is a belief that thoughts and actions are really the same. You may not be aware you believe this, but it lies at the back of your mind and guides how you feel and what you do.

One form of this muddle is the idea of *moral thought–action fusion*: it's just as bad to think something as it is to do it.

Another form of the muddle is the idea of *likelihood thought–action fusion*: if you think about something it's much more likely to happen. So if you think about something bad happening to someone, somehow that will make it happen, and it'll be your fault for thinking it in the first place. And this leads on to the compulsion (because you feel responsible for everything) to make sure that it doesn't!

Control

People don't often talk about Freud these days, but some of his ideas about OCD still seem relevant. Freud argued that sometimes when bad things happen to people, over which they have no real control, they start to think in an almost magical way to give themselves the feeling of being in control. For example, a child can't usually influence whether his parents divorce or not – but he might be so desperate to stop them separating that he starts doing things that give him a sense of being in control – lining his toys up in exactly the same way every day, or washing his hands perfectly. Even though this will have no real effect, it will make him *feel* that he is able to do something, and in the short term this will help him to feel better.

For example, a young man called Steve who developed problems remembers thinking, 'I must put all the soldiers in an exact line – if I can get it right then Daddy won't shout at Mummy tonight.' Sometimes something similar seems to be happening with OCD. You can't control the bad things in your life, so you try to control other things – the tidiness of the living room, or whether the cups are all facing the same way in the kitchen. These things don't really make a difference to what happens in your life, but the 'magical thinking' gives you the illusion that you can be in control.

When we think about Sally and Derek we can see how some of these ideas might be working. Sally certainly has very strong ideas that she is responsible for everything, and that if anything did go wrong she would be to blame. Derek thinks he is a terrible person for having these thoughts (*thoughts about thoughts* and *moral thought–action fusion*); and he thinks that he might carry them out and has to take steps to prevent this (*likelihood thought–action fusion*).

Part 2 looks at each of these problems with thinking and behaving in more detail, and sets out some ideas about how you can change them. But before doing so, it's worth saying a bit about how all of this affects the people around you.

3

What About Your Friends and Family?

There is no doubt that when OCD gets bad it can have a very big effect on the people around you. For instance, one person was unable to let her husband and children into the house unless they took off all their clothes at the back door. Another actually hoovered her husband before she would let him into the house. You may get very irritable and angry with partners and children who don't realise how important your obsessions are to you and might put things away in the wrong place, for example, or not put them away at all.

It's very difficult for a partner of someone with OCD to know what to do. Should they give in to the obsessions, and do what their partner wants? This will keep the peace in the house, but it means that they'll have to carry out some pretty odd and time-consuming tasks. It also means that you'll have less motivation to get better, and in the long term it can contribute to making the obsessions worse.

So should the partner resist the obsessions and just carry on as normal? This will make life very difficult for you and will almost certainly lead to arguments and tears.

All of this can place a very great strain on partnerships, with increasing anger and misunderstanding on both sides. It can also place a very great strain on children, not just because a parent is behaving in strange ways and getting angry, but because the child may learn to become obsessional, too.

A good first step for the partner (and even older children) of someone with OCD is to learn a bit about the condition. Perhaps give them this book to read. Then, while you are taking part in this programme, tell your partner what you're trying to do. Sometimes they'll be able to help, giving you encouragement and pushing you on a bit. If you both decide that you'd like to do this, then it's important for your partner to be guided in the programme by you, and not to force the pace. On the other hand, if things have got so bad that you can't really talk about your OCD without getting into an argument, it's probably better for your partner not to be too involved. Just letting him or her know that you are working on the problem yourself might relieve the tension and make them feel a bit better about how things are going.

If you don't have a partner, you could ask a relative or friend to help you in this way. Again, if your OCD has been a cause of friction just let the people around you know that you are working on a pro-gramme of self-help.

Part 2: COPING WITH OBSESSIONS AND COMPULSIONS

Even if OCD has taken a terrible hold of your life, the good news is that there's hope! Drug treatments, particularly the newer drugs, can make a big difference to OCD. And psychological treatments, although sometimes hard work, are very effective.

The first chapter in this section will look briefly at drug treatments for OCD, and the next two will go on to describe in some detail two related kinds of psychological treatment.

4

Drug Treatments for OCD

A number of drug treatments are very useful for OCD. Many of the relatively new drugs called SSRIs (short for 'selective serotonin reuptake inhibitors') can be very helpful in treating the symptoms, and at least one of the older tricyclic anti-depressants, clomipramine, can also be very effective. If you are interested in trying medication, then your GP will advise you on the best drug to suit you. Medication can be particularly useful if the OCD is dragging your mood down and making you feel very low.

Here are some key points about medication:

- Medication for OCD is normally prescribed by your GP, or by a psychiatrist if you are seeing one. It cannot be bought over the counter at the chemist.

- There are different variations of the SSRIs, and although they're broadly similar, different ones suit different people. Or you may be someone who responds better to the tricyclic type of medication. If you don't respond well to the first one you try, tell your doctor; it's almost certainly worth trying another.

• Medication can take as long as two to four weeks to produce beneficial changes. Usually the side effects come before the therapeutic effects, and it's tempting to give up. But hang on! Normally the side effects will wear off after a while and the beneficial effects will start to kick in.

• It's important not to stop taking the medication as soon as you notice that you are feeling better. It's usually recommended to keep taking the medication for some time to get things to stabilise. Stopping the medication too quickly can make it more likely that the problems will come back.

• If you do decide to stop, either because the medication isn't working or because you have been feeling better for a while, don't stop suddenly. Wean yourself off the dose slowly, over a few weeks, and always discuss this with your doctor first.

• For some people, taking medication seems to do the trick on its own; for others, it can be very useful together with psychological therapy

– for example, it can make it easier for you to carry out some of the steps described in the following sections of this book.

5

Behavioural Treatment for OCD: Exposure and Response Prevention

Exposure and response prevention (ERP) has proved to be very effective. This treatment has two parts, working respectively on the obsessions and the compulsions.

How does exposure and response prevention work?

We've talked about how you come into contact with something that makes you anxious (the obsession) and go straight to the compulsion, to make yourself feel better as soon as possible. But this keeps the cycle of obsession and compulsion going. The idea of exposure and response prevention is that, to break this cycle, you allow yourself to come into contact with the obsessions, and resist the temptation to carry out the compulsions.

So the first part, exposure, means *starting to let yourself come into contact with the things that make you feel anxious.*

The second part is *response prevention* – the idea is that when you do things that make you anxious, *you do **not** carry out the compulsion.* In other words, you do nothing to make yourself feel better!

Although this sounds very harsh, after a while the anxiety starts to wear off. Exactly the same principle is used in the treatment of phobias: for example, someone who was frightened of spiders would be encouraged to look at pictures or words about spiders, and eventually to look at a live spider – even hold one if they felt like it! When you're exposed to things that make you feel anxious, and hang on in there without running away or carrying out your usual compulsion, then the anxiety starts to wear off. This is true for phobias and for OCD.

Understanding anxiety

Before going on, look at the diagram on the next page (Figure 1). What normally happens when you expose yourself to something that triggers an obsession is that you get very anxious (point 1 on the graph). When you carry out the compulsion, this anxiety is reduced, very quickly and very effectively (point 2). Many people fear that if they don't carry out the compulsion, then their anxiety may never lessen, or may even carry on going up (point 3). But in fact what happens is that the anxiety stays high for a while, and then, *without your needing to do anything*, it will start to come down, and will eventually fall to exactly the same level it would have been if you had carried out the compulsion (point 4). This means that over time you will start to recover from the anxiety without needing to do the compulsion at all.

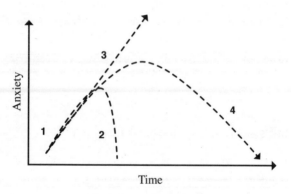

Figure 1: The course of anxiety over time in obsessive compulsive disorder

To summarise:

1. Encounter with obsessional trigger – anxiety goes up.

2. When compulsion is carried out, anxiety decreases rapidly.

3. Fear that, if the compulsion is not carried out, anxiety will increase indefinitely.

4. In fact, anxiety decreases over time without compulsive activity.

Now, normally people find it very difficult to carry out the exposure, and it is important to make sure that you don't try to do too much too soon. Although occasionally drastic measures are called for, it's much better to expose yourself in small and manageable steps – otherwise you may find that the experience is so horrible you just don't want to go on with it.

SUDs and how they can help you

Let's talk about SUDs, a jargony acronym that stands for *subjective units of discomfort*. It's a measure you can use to keep track of how you're feeling and which can help you to plan your treatment. The SUDs rating just means 'how bad you feel'. It can vary in content from person to person, with a mixture of anxiety, anger, agitation and misery. Only you know exactly what it's like for you. But however you feel, it should be possible to make a rough judgment of how bad it is. SUDs can be rated from 0 to 100 – 100 is the worst that you can imagine feeling, and 0 is completely fine.

Now – back to exposure and response prevention…

Planning your exposure programme

1. First, write out a list of all the different things that make you anxious.

2. Now write out a list of the compulsions that you carry out as a result. Put these in order of how badly you need to do them, starting with the least bad.

3. Rate each one using SUDs – i.e. rate how bad you'd feel, on a scale of 0–100, if you didn't do it.

4. Make a copy of the form opposite to help you write this down. If your OCD is quite compli-cated, it might be easier to start just with one problem at a time.

Things that make me anxious

1. . . . .

2. . . . .

3. . . . .

Things I have to do, in order of SUDs

1. . . . .

2. . . . .

3. . . . .

5. Now the task is to expose yourself to the thing that makes you anxious without doing anything to make it better.

6. Choose something in the range of 30–40 SUDs; that is, something that will make you

feel a bit bad, but won't be too much for you to manage.

7. Decide exactly what you are going to do, or what you are going to expose yourself to, and then *do it*.

8. Rate your SUDs straight away and take a note of how high the rating is.

9. Now wait for five minutes, and rate your SUDs again.

10. Keep a note every five or ten minutes of how bad you are feeling. Although you may find that within the first few minutes the rating goes up, after a while it will start to come down as your anxiety starts to wear off.

11. You could draw a form based on the one opposite to help keep track of your anxiety levels.

Date and time	Exposure and response prevention task	SUDs on first exposure	SUDs after 5 mins	SUDs after 10 mins	SUDS after 30 mins	SUDs after 1 hr

Here is an example of how Sally used these forms.

Things that make me anxious

1. Letting Becca touch anything before she has a bath when she comes in

2. Putting washing in machine when it might be dirty

3. Seeing Becca's clothes on the floor when she takes them off

4. Letting Ben get in the bath with Becca

5. Thinking about contamination

Things I have to do, in order of SUDs

1. Prewash washing machine before I put clothes in

   SUDs 20

2. Put Becca's clothes in a plastic bag when she takes them off and wash them straight away

   SUDs 20

---

3. Stop Ben getting in the bath (I know he'd love to)

   SUDs 40

4. Take Becca straight upstairs when she gets home

   SUDs 50

5. Do all of the above!

Sally's exposure and response prevention record

Date and time	Exposure and response prevention task	SUDs on first exposure	SUDs after 5 mins	SUDs after 10 min	SUDs after 30 min	SUDs after 1 hr
Mon 2.15	Didn't prewash washing machine and put Becca's clothes in anyway	20	50	20	5	5
Tues 2.15	Didn't prewash washing machine and put Becca's clothes in	10	60!	10	5	5

Weds 1.45	Put Becca's clothes in laundry basket not special bag	40 (really want to wash it now)	20	20	20	20
Weds 2.15	Didn't prewash washing machine and put Becca's clothes in	5 (thinking about laundry basket instead!)	5	5	5	5
Fri 2.15	Let Ben get in bath!!	70	80	70	30	30

The trouble with exposure and response prevention is that it can make you feel very bad indeed, particularly at the beginning when you aren't confident it will work, and not used to tolerating the horrible feelings of anxiety that arise. But if you can make yourself go through with this programme, you'll start to feel much better, and you'll feel much less need to carry out the compulsions. It's not easy – but it does work!

Which types of OCD respond best to this approach?

Exposure and response prevention is particularly useful in the treatment of cleaning and checking types of OCD. It's also helpful for problems with order and symmetry, hoarding and slowness, but it's slightly harder to apply them to these problems. If this applies to you and you're reading this book on your own, you may find that you'll need some advice from a professional about how to go about it.

Cognitive Treatment for OCD: How to Tackle Intrusive Thoughts and 'Thoughts About Thoughts'

As discussed in Part 1, some people are very troubled by intrusive thoughts even though they don't carry out obvious or extensive compulsions. These people tend to avoid situations which might trigger the thoughts.

Some examples of intrusive thoughts

Derek had intrusive thoughts about stabbing people when he saw knives, and had at least one intrusive thought about his grandson.

Another example is Lucy, who had very troubling thoughts that she might harm her young children. When they were in the bath she had the thought, 'I might drown them', and had an image of herself holding them underwater. Lucy had to stop bathing her children, and even found it difficult to cuddle them sometimes in case she thought of harming them.

Why do we have these thoughts?

Psychologists studying this problem realised that when they asked people who weren't troubled by obsessions whether they ever had strange thoughts that just came into their minds, almost everyone said yes. When psychologists looked at the kinds of thoughts that people reported, there were a number of common themes: these were, typically, ideas or images about sex, particularly inappropriate or unwelcome ones; and ideas or images of violence or harm, particularly of harm coming to oneself and other people, or of causing harm to other people. Although it's strange, it seems that it's simply in the nature of human thinking that we do think these things. The fact that we think them, however, *really doesn't mean that we want to do them*.

As you've seen, it's 'normal' for people to experience very similar thoughts to the ones that are common in obsessions. Why then do some people have these thoughts without developing obsessions, while others are so troubled by them?

Why do intrusive thoughts become obsessions?

The answer seems to lie in the attitude people have to their thoughts. For example, one mother might have an image of herself harming her children and think, 'Oh yuk, fancy thinking such a weird thought, I certainly don't want to do that!' But another might think, 'Oh my God, what a terrible thing to think – if I'm thinking that, it must mean that I want to do it. How can I think that? I must be a terrible, evil person.' In the first case, the mother would have the thought, but wouldn't worry too much about it, and wouldn't have to do anything as a result. But in the second case, the mother would worry a great deal. She'd start to watch her thoughts, to make sure that she wasn't thinking them. She'd struggle to dismiss the thoughts and get them out of her mind. She'd also start to avoid situations where she might have the thoughts, and where she fears she might harm the children. However, psychologists have realised that there is a very strange and unfortunate truth about thoughts: the more you try to stop having them, the worse and more frequent they get. So the more the second mother tries not to have the 'bad' thoughts, the more she has them.

You can demonstrate this effect to yourself with any kind of thought. For instance, for the next two minutes, try to make sure that you do not think about pink elephants…

How did it go? Did you think of pink elephants at all? It would be very unusual if you hadn't! The effect of trying *not* to think something brings it into your mind, rather than keeping it out.

The unfortunate effect of this is that as the thoughts become more frequent you make more and more harsh judgements about yourself. The more, and the worse, the thoughts are, the more you feel this 'proves' you are bad, or are going to carry them out.

Another way of thinking about this is that the thoughts that become obsessions are usually associated with areas of life where you have very high standards, so that the presence of such a thought goes against everything you believe in about the world or yourself. For instance, blasphemous thoughts are much more common in very religious people, to whom such thoughts are repugnant.

You may also think you are going mad, and that these thoughts are the beginning of the decline into total madness and institutionalisation.

What can be done about intrusive thoughts?

The first step is for you to think very carefully

about the explanation above, and to realise that *it is normal to have extraordinary thoughts*, and that they don't mean that you are bad, mad, dangerous or anything else other than normal. In fact, you're probably more troubled by the thoughts than other people would be because you have high standards for yourself and the world, not because there is something wrong with you.

The next step is to *stop fighting the thoughts*. When they come into your mind, instead of panicking and thinking, 'Oh no, I mustn't think that, I must stop', try to keep calm. Remind yourself that it's OK to have these thoughts, and just let them drift through your mind. If you feel able, you could even try something similar to the exposure technique described in Chapter 5. Set aside ten minutes or half an hour a day, and make yourself have the thoughts deliberately. Don't try to avoid them or send them away. Even though it will make you very anxious and uncomfortable at first, you'll find that you somehow get used to the thoughts, and that they'll stop seeming so frightening.

Finally, if the intrusive thoughts have made you avoid things, start to work with the avoidance, by gradually making yourself do things you've stopped doing, or go to places you've stopped going.

You'll find that as you tackle the thoughts in this way you'll become less worried about them and they'll start to occur much less often. You may still have them from time to time, because almost everyone does. But hopefully you can just let them drift through your mind without taking too much notice!

But what if I carry the thoughts out?

Many of the intrusive thoughts described concern the thought or image of you doing something. This might be causing harm to someone else, or to yourself, or doing something completely socially unacceptable. It's very important to realise that these *obsessional thoughts are never carried out*.[1]

Try thinking about this in the following way:

Most people believe that there is a direct link between thoughts and action, like this:

$$\text{Thought} = \text{Action}$$

But in fact there's another part of the chain that most of us are not aware of: in order to do something,

---

[1] *Of course, sometimes people do carry out horrible actions, as we're all only too aware from reports in the media. But people who do carry out these actions have different problems from the ones that we're talking about here. For those people, there's no sense that these thoughts are alien and unwanted, and although they may resist them this may be more from a fear of the consequences than because they genuinely feel that they are wrong.*

we have to *intend* to do it. So the diagram should actually look like this:

$$\text{Thought} + \text{Intention} = \text{Action}$$

No matter what you think about, it's only the introduction of the intention – actually *meaning* to do it, planning it, etc. – that leads to action; it is *not the thought itself.*

Now, it's very easy for psychologists to say this, and much harder for you to believe it, particularly if you've always taken steps to make sure that you don't put your intrusive thoughts into practice. But the only way to convince yourself that you can have the thoughts and not carry them out is to start to let yourself think them, and to put yourself into situations where you might have them.

The central message in all of this is that –

Thoughts are just thoughts!

– that is, things that go on in your mind. There's a great temptation to think that all thoughts are meaningful and significant; and that having a thought can make something come true. But they aren't. You can think anything you like in your head without it meaning anything or having any effect on the world at all.

Remember: *Thoughts are just thoughts!*

Derek's story (continued)

Derek finally saw a therapist and told her about his intrusive thoughts. The therapist explained that such thoughts are normal and assured him that he wouldn't carry them out. The therapist was so sure about this that she got Derek to bring a kitchen knife to the session. She encouraged Derek to hold the knife when he was sitting with her and to allow himself to have the thought 'This is for stabbing.' At first Derek refused to do this – he was too worried that he would use the knife. But the therapist seemed confident. Eventually he allowed himself to hold the knife, and to have the thought and even the mental image of himself stabbing her.

Eventually he started to realise that no matter what he thought in his head, he really wasn't going to stab her!

The therapist also encouraged Derek to get the knives and scissors out at home, and to leave them in the kitchen. Gaining confidence from what happened in the therapy sessions, Derek started to invite people into his home again, and was able to cook for them. After a while, because he wasn't worrying about them so much, the thoughts just seemed to die down. Although he still had them occasionally, he was able to say, 'Oh – those ridiculous thoughts again' and not to worry!

Dealing with 'thoughts about thoughts' or 'metacognitions'

It's bad enough just to have obsessional thoughts, but there also seems to be an extra layer to the problem. You've seen how, when people experience obsessional thoughts, they think they must mean them, or really want to carry them out. These 'thoughts about thoughts' are also called 'metacognitions'. Another very common type of metacognition concerns the idea of responsibility and blame – I'll be a 'bad person' if I don't do my best to prevent harm coming to someone, or if I'm not watching out for problems all the time.

Very often, if someone is helped to cope with this 'extra layer' of metacognition then the obsessions and compulsions also get better. So we need a way of helping to identify the metacognitions, and trying to change them.

The first step is to keep a diary of your thoughts, writing down exactly what is going through your mind. On the opposite page is an example from Sally's diary (again, draw a blank version of this form in your notebook to complete this exercise).

Once you've learned to identify the thoughts, the next step is to learn to challenge them. There are a number of questions you can ask yourself to help with this.

- *Is there any evidence for this thought?*

- *Is there any evidence against it?*

- *Would it stand up in a court of law?*

- *What would I say to a friend who thought like this?*

- *What would a friend say to me about it?*

- *What are the effects of thinking as I do?*

- *How can I test this out to show myself that the thoughts are false?*

Sally's attempt to use these questions would look like this:

Thought: I'm a really irresponsible, bad mother.

Evidence for: Can't really think of anything (apart from the letting them do things – but then I know they ought to really).

Example from Sally's diary for identifying and challenging metacognitions

Date and time	Obsessional thoughts	Metacognition	Emotion	Challenge to metacognition
Monday 2.00	I let Becca play with Sam this morning. I know his mother doesn't worry about his clothes – she might have got wee on her or worse	If I was a good mother I'd be able to keep Becca away from situations like this – I'm a really irresponsible, bad mother. If anything happens to her it's my fault	Tense, worried, guilty	

Evidence against: I know that I do care a lot, and I try my best for them. Apart from the whole awful business of obsessions I do take good care of them. I play with them, and make sure they have a nice home.

Would it stand up in a court of law? It feels wrong to say it, but even I can see that a court of law wouldn't condemn me for letting my daughter play!

What would I say to a friend who thought like this? I think I'd say, don't be silly – just because you let her go out to play doesn't mean you're a bad mother. It just seems different when it's me!

What would a friend say to me? I know that my friends, and Martin, think I'm a good mother, and also think I'm silly to worry so much.

What are the effects of thinking as I do? Well, I suppose when I feel irresponsible and bad I get more upset, and that makes me more worried and more obsessional. I think I lose perspective even more.

How can I test out whether I'm a bad mother or not? I could ask people what they think of me. I could also remind myself to look at the children! They both seem happy and energetic, and they both seem very affectionate towards me!

Having asked herself these questions, Sally can now go back to the form and complete the last column.

Example from Sally's diary for identifying and challenging metacognitions

Date and time	Obsessional thoughts	Metacognition	Emotion	Challenge to metacognition
Monday 2.00	I let Becca play with Sam this morning. I know his mother doesn't worry about his clothes – she might have got wee on her – or worse	If I was a good mother I'd be able to keep Becca away from situations like this – I'm a really irresponsible, bad mother. If anything happens to her it's my fault	Tense, worried, guilty	I know I take good care of my children, and they are happy and doing well. Doing the obsessions actually makes me worse, not better!

Additional techniques for dealing with ideas of responsibility and blame

You can do a similar kind of thing to deal with ideas that you're totally responsible for things that might happen. What is the evidence that you're totally and solely responsible for what might happen? What is the evidence that other people may play a part in things?

Make a list of all the people who are involved in the things you're worried about – yourself, your partner, the electricity board, the gas board, other drivers on the road, careless cyclists or pedestrians. How much does each of you realistically contribute to what might happen? How can it be up to you to control what other people do? In some cases you may be worried about what insurance companies call 'acts of God' – floods, for example. How can these be your responsibility?

There are another two thoughts that are common for people with very strong ideas of responsibility. One is that if something bad happened and you'd failed to prevent it, you'd be guilty, *even if what happened wasn't your fault*. The second is that *even if something is incredibly unlikely*, it's still your responsibility to make sure it doesn't happen, and to take extreme steps to make sure of this. So it's very difficult to take the risk of stopping the compulsions.

But although it's so difficult, try to ask yourself some of the questions above – what would a friend say to you about this? Would a court of law agree it was your fault?

Keep telling yourself that responsibility for these things doesn't rest with you – and you'll eventually start to believe it!

Thought-action fusion

Sometimes people can get in a great muddle about the relationship between thinking and action, and believe that if you think something it's as bad as doing it, or that it might happen. It's important to go back to the idea that *thoughts are just thoughts*.

Likelihood thought-action fusion

If you're afraid that thinking something might make it happen, try looking out of the window at the building next door. Think about this falling down. Get a really strong picture in your mind that this will happen. Now look again. I'll bet anything you like that the building is still standing. This is the same with any other kind of prediction.

Remember: *Thinking is only something that goes on in your head. It doesn't have an effect on the real world.*

Moral thought-action fusion

If you think that you're bad to have a particular thought, try looking at the earlier section on 'What Can Be Done About Intrusive Thoughts?' (page 48). This explains the idea that thoughts are just thoughts, and you aren't bad to think them.

You could try another experiment. Imagine your neighbour is unwell and needs some shopping done for her. Think about doing it. Does this make you a good person? Will she be grateful? The answer is obvious. In order to be good and helpful you have to *do* the action, not just think about it. The same is exactly true for bad thoughts. These thoughts cannot harm anyone, and you aren't bad to have them!

Control

Sometimes people carry out compulsions because it gives them a feeling that they can control bad things going on around them, even when they can't. Sometimes these compulsions can act as a way of avoiding tackling problems – instead of meeting the real problem head-on, you feel so anxious that you retreat into obsessions and compulsions. Like many aspects of OCD, this can make you feel better while you are doing it, but it doesn't help much in the longer term.

More effective in the longer term is to try to face the anxiety that the real problem is causing, and see if there is anything that can be done. It may be that once you've faced the problem there are other people around who could help, too – your GP, a counsellor, the Citizens Advice Bureau, for example, might be good starting places.

A Last Word of Encouragement

When you start to make changes in your behaviour, there is often a kind of 'time lag' – you can force yourself to change what you *do*, and train yourself to *think* differently – but you still *feel* the same. It's tempting at this point to give up. But if you carry on with the changes, *your feelings will eventually catch up*, and the new ways of doing things will seem much more natural and right.

In summary, please remember that although OCD can seem overwhelming and incomprehensible, it need not be quite so bad as all that. We *can* make sense of obsessions and compulsions, and there *are* things that you can do to try to tackle them. It's rarely easy – sometimes changing what you do, particularly if you've been doing it for a long time, can be very demanding and can make you feel very bad. But as you start to make changes they tend to get easier, and if you can stick at it you'll quickly start to feel a lot better.

Good luck!

Other Things That Might Help

This book has provided you with an introduction to the problems caused by obsessive compulsive disorder and what you can do to overcome them. Some people will find that this is all they need to do to see a big improvement, while others may feel that they need a bit more information and help, and in that case there are some longer and more detailed self-help books around. Using self-help books, particularly those based on cognitive behavioural therapy (CBT), have been found to be particularly effective in the treatment of anxiety-related problems. Ask your GP if there's a Books on Prescription scheme running in your area – if there isn't, the following book is recommended:

Overcoming Obsessive Compulsive Disorder by David Veale and Rob Willson, published by Constable & Robinson

Sometimes the self-help approach works better if you have someone supporting you. Ask your GP if there's anyone at the surgery who would be able to work through your self-help book with you. Some surgeries have Graduate Mental Health Workers who would be able to help in this way, or who might offer general support. He or she is likely to be able to spend more time with you than your GP and may offer follow-up appointments.

For some people, a self-help approach may not be enough. If this is the case for you, don't despair – there are other kinds of help available.

Talk to your GP – make an appointment to talk through the different treatment options on offer to you. Your GP can refer you to an NHS therapist for cognitive behavioural therapy – most places now have CBT available on the NHS, although there can be a considerable waiting list. Don't be put off if you've not found working through a CBT-based self-help manual right for you – talking to a therapist can make a big difference. If an NHS therapist isn't available in your area or you'd prefer not to wait to see one, ask your GP to recommend a private therapist.

Although CBT is widely recommended for obsessive compulsive disorder there are many other kinds of therapy available that you could also discuss with your GP.

Medication can be very helpful for some people and sometimes a combination of medication and psychological therapy can work wonders. However, you need to discuss this form of treatment and any possible side effects with your doctor to work out whether it's right for you.

The following organisations offer help and advice on OCD and you may find them a useful source of information:

British Association for Behavioural and Cognitive Psychotherapies (BABCP)

☎: 0161 705 4304

Email: babcp@babcp.com

Website: www.babcp.org.uk

Provides contact details for therapists in your area, both NHS and private.

Mind

☎: 0300 123 3393

Website: www.mind.org.uk

No Panic UK

Helpline: 0844 967 4848

Website: www.nopanic.org.uk

OCD Action

Help and information line: 0845 390 6232

Website: www.ocdaction.org.uk

An Introduction to Coping with Depression

2nd Edition

Lee Brosan and Brenda Hogan

ISBN: 978-1-47214-021-0

Practical support for how to overcome depression and low mood

Depression is the predominant mental health condition worldwide, affecting millions of people each year. But it can be treated effectively with cognitive behavioural therapy (CBT).

Written by experienced practitioners, this introductory book explains what depression is and how it makes you feel. It will help you to understand your symptoms and is ideal as an immediate coping strategy and as a preliminary to fuller therapy.

You will learn:
· How depression develops and what keeps it going
· How to spot and challenge thoughts that maintain your depression
· Problem solving and balanced thinking skills

An Introduction to Coping with Extreme Emotions:

A Guide to Borderline or Emotionally Unstable Personality Disorder

Lee Brosan and Amanda Spong

ISBN: 978-1-47213-732-6

Learn how to cope with extreme or unstable emotions

Many people suffer from extreme emotions with around 2% of people being diagnosed with Borderline Personality Disorder. It is a very troubling condition which causes abnormal and unstable behaviour including overwhelming feelings of distress and anger, which may lead to self-harming, damage or destruction of relationships and, at times, loss of contact with reality.

Through clinically proven dialectical behaviour therapy (DBT) techniques, this book will help you to control your extreme emotions.

You will learn:
· The symptoms of personality disorder
· Different ways of coping with overwhelming emotions
· How to increase your emotional resilience from day to day

The Complete CBT Guide
for Anxiety

Roz Shafran, Lee Brosan, Peter Cooper

ISBN: 978-1-84901-896-8

A highly respectable and authoritative self-help guide on all the anxiety disorders: generalised anxiety disorder, health anxiety, panic, phobias, social anxiety, OCD.

Edited by three leading CBT clinicians in the UK, this comprehensive guide offers individual CBT-based treatments for a wide range of anxiety problems. Each individual treatment reflects current the treatment in the UK for that anxiety disorder and is written by the clinician responsible for developing that treatment in the first place.

An ideal resource not only for those experiencing anxiety problems, but CBT therapists and IAPT workers.

An Introduction to Coping with Stress

2nd Edition

Lee Brosan

ISBN: 978-1-4721-4019-7

Practical support for how to overcome stress

We all know what stress feels like, and indeed what it feels like when we have too much stress in our lives. Too much stress can have a negative impact on us, almost without our noticing it. It can affect our family life, friendships and other relationships, our work life and our physical and emotional wellbeing.

Written by an experienced practitioner and author of the popular self-help title Overcoming Stress, this introductory book can help you if stress has become a problem, using cognitive behavioural therapy (CBT) strategies to:

· Help you recognise what happens when you are under stress
· Change how you feel, think and act in order to regain
a more balanced outlook
· Manage everyday life more effectively